Acknowledgement

I would like to give a special Thank you to Kelly Cleckler for copy editing my book. Thank you so much Kelly.

Virtual Reality and Augmented Reality Safety Rules

Mohammed Azzam

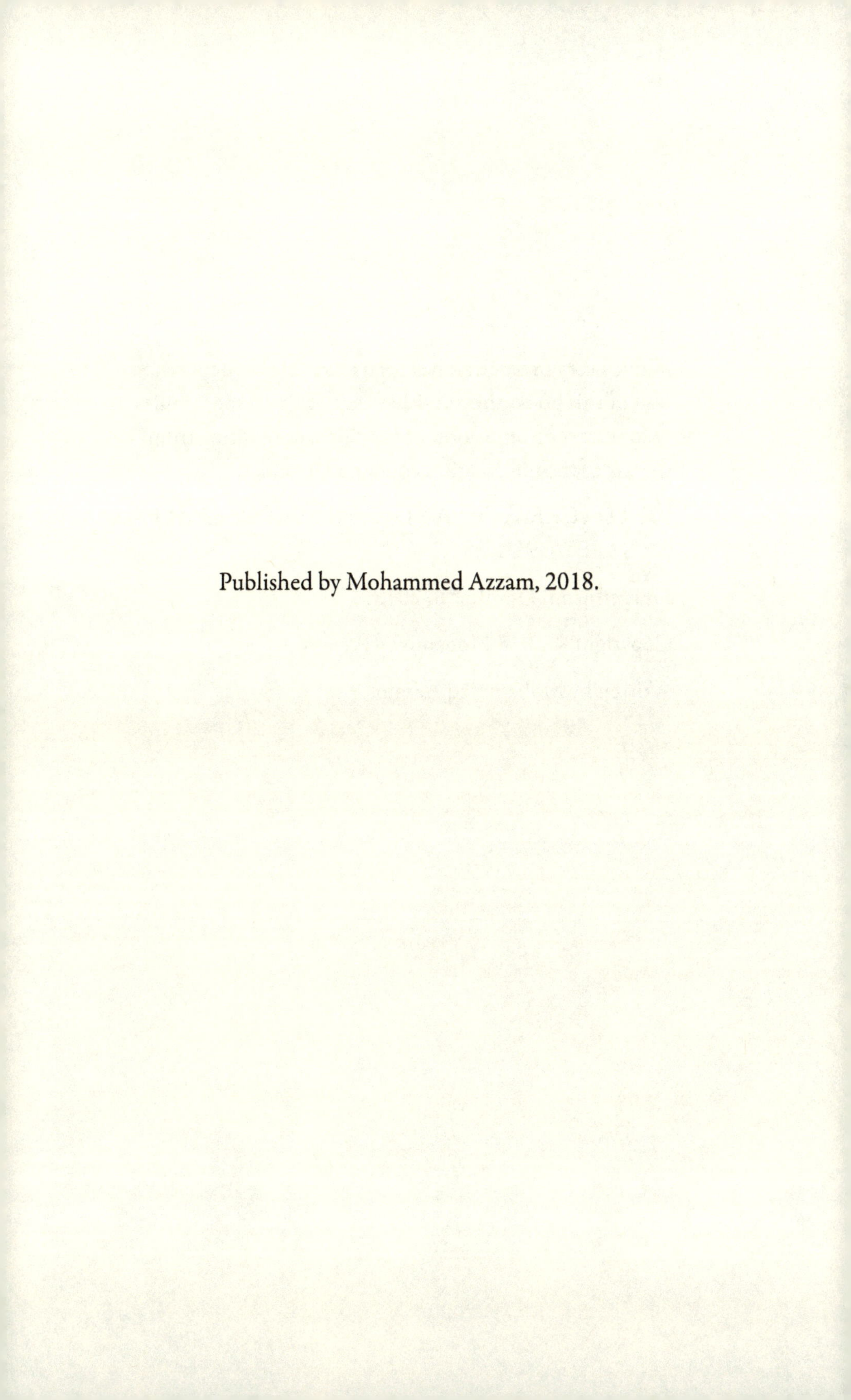Published by Mohammed Azzam, 2018.

VIRTUAL REALITY AND AUGMENTED REALITY SAFETY RULES

First edition. October 6, 2018.

Written by Mohammed Azzam.

Also by Mohammed Azzam

Inflation and Variable Interest
Virtual Reality and Augmented Reality Safety Rules
Known Facts of Time Travel

Watch for more at https://books2read.com/ap/
R3Lm35/Mohammed-Azzam.

Preface

Can you, virtual reality user or augmented reality user play your favorite game after drinking a large bottle of tequila? This book discusses the golden safety rules for you as a virtual reality or augmented reality user from best practice point of view not from manufacturing point of view! It tells you what those virtual reality or augmented reality companies won't tell you or they will lose money if they told you! But someone must tell you! If you are interested, you may continue reading:

To keep this book as simple as possible we will adopt the Hollywood style version of virtual reality and augmented reality that's to say we will discuss those golden safety rules as a Hollywood director would discuss them in a documentary movie for the sake of simplicity only, we will talk here about virtual reality games and augmented reality games only for the sake of simplicity too, leaving virtual reality media or augmented reality media a side, as those can only be judged right if content has been watched or seen! The previously mentioned virtual reality media means movies or sports etc. while augmented reality media means press or books etc.

This book adopts best practice point of view and discusses how it conflicts with software engineering point of view or in other words Manufacturing point of view, actually this book is about "Virtual Reality and Augmented Reality Timeline Theory" which is a social theory this book adopts, don't worry this book is as simple as watching a movie, so we will start in the next chapter by a Hollywood style definition for both virtual reality and augmented reality, but they are true definitions.

This book introduces a social theory called "Humanity Timeline Theory" in part two: let's consider an LCD, yes that LCD you use at home to watch your favorite programs and serials! Let's look at what it consists of? It's made of a screen which is glass, glass is made of sand. Also, it is made of some chips which are made of silicon, silicon is sand. Your LCD includes some printed circuits that's made of copper and plastic, plastic is a polymer that's made of oil. This concludes that the main raw material that your LCD is made of are: sand, copper, oil and may be some gold!

Don't you think that this raw material isn't there on earth since the stone age?

Yes, those raw material used to make your own LCD particularly were on Earth since the stone age, so why that stone age man couldn't make himself an LCD or did he make himself an LCD, but we don't know? This book answers this question. If you are interested, you may start reading part two.

PART ONE

Virtual Reality and Augmented Reality Definition

How will a Hollywood director explain what's virtual reality to his movie's star actor or star actress?

Virtual reality is the new picture quality technology that makes watching an almost natural 3D view is possible, so the audience can watch the scene as if it's really happening at the current moment and as exactly as your co-worker who is the cameraman has seen it.

For example, this what should Francis Lawrence tell Jennifer Lawrence to describe virtual reality if he is going to shoot a virtual reality movie! Yes, that's true because the whole damn movie is about Jennifer Lawrence act, besides the audience here is a passive audience who are 3DoF users because nobody will go to theater to run marathon!

That's right, the type of audience for a virtual reality movie is a passive audience because everybody wants to watch a movie and relax, really 6DoF virtual reality movies users who are called active audience is not accepted in theaters, those are for gyms because they really do aerobics.

Yes, 6DoF virtual reality movies or 6DoF virtual reality music is not cinema, it's aerobics. It can be used as a computer monitored aerobics program so your computer can tell if you have exercised right or wrong? Enough talking about passive audience, the rest of this book is about virtual reality games users or augmented reality games users who are called active audience.

How will a Hollywood director explain what's augmented reality to his movie's star actor or star actress?

Just recall "The Terminator" (1984) movie starring Schwarzenegger if you have watched this movie and if you have not watch it then I recommend you watch it, you'll notice one of The Terminator cool features is that his eyes has the ability to write some information about what he sees right now, on the view he currently sees.

This process of writing some information or drawing a picture on the view that's being seen right now is called augmented reality by definition! Yes, these eyes are called scientifically an augmented reality implanted eyes.

For short, just recall that scene when Sarah Conner is running out of the night club and The Terminator is following her, it's about 35 minutes since the beginning of the movie, you should notice that The Terminator eyes has such ability. The Terminator is a famous character that uses augmented reality extensively actually.

Literally, anything you can put on a paper you can put within lenses using augmented reality.

Virtual Reality and Augmented Reality Timeline Theory

As you can conclude from previous chapter, virtual reality and augmented reality are both totally different media approaches. Virtual reality is all about motion picture like movies, sports or TV shows etc. while augmented reality is all about written words like newspapers, journalism, novels or press etc.

A major difference between virtual reality and augmented reality is about the user timeline, how each of virtual reality and augmented reality treat the user timeline? Now, virtual reality and augmented reality timeline theory is as follows:

Each of virtual reality and augmented reality treat the user timeline differently, virtual reality user can't watch or deal or even feel his own current timeline, he can watch a historical event in his timeline but not the current moment of his timeline, So literally he's blind!

Meanwhile augmented reality user can only watch or deal or feel his own current timeline!

The paragraph above is a social theory called "Virtual Reality and Augmented Reality Timeline Theory" and that paragraph is about the single human timeline while the talking about the broad human history timeline as a whole is called "Humanity Timeline Theory"! For more information please read part two.

We can say that augmented reality is more precise than virtual reality, and I mean by the term "precise" is how accurate is the seen view, in comparison to the user's current timeline at the current moment, and that's the meaning used for the term "precise" through this book!

How to Choose Between Virtual Reality and Augmented Reality?

How will a Hollywood director explain how to choose between virtual reality and augmented reality to his movie's star actor or star actress?

Just think of the audience and ask yourself:

Do they need to watch or deal or even feel their timeline to feel the drama and interact with the story line? If the answer is no, so augmented reality is unnecessary.

Do they need to watch or deal or even feel their timeline at the same moment the scene is on screen? If the answer is no, so augmented reality is unnecessary.

For short usually the movie's scenario or story line has nothing to do with the audience timeline, it's a story-telling movie that has nothing to do with the audience!

So augmented reality usually is not necessary for making a movie, virtual reality is quite enough.

As you can see the major difference is about the user timeline, is it part of your project or not? If it is then how accurate you need that timeline? If you need it very accurate so badly then go for augmented reality because it is the only way.

Beside this user timeline difference, there is media difference which is both virtual reality and augmented reality are both totally different media approaches. virtual reality is all about motion picture, while augmented reality is all about press and publishing.

Virtual reality media is motion picture.

Augmented reality media is press or publishing.

What encourages press or publishing to be augmented reality media? Firstly, let us find an answer to the question: Will an augmented reality movie be available soon? As I explained augmented reality before, shooting locations cannot be fulfilled in augmented reality! For example, if the movie scene is about an actor is sitting on a coach, there is no guarantee that the augmented reality user will be looking at a coach while that scene is playing! In other words, say the user may be watching a car, right then the actor will be sitting on a car's roof! So, it is impossible to produce an augmented reality movie. I have worked at a production site for seven years and you can take my word for that, no shooting locations no movies. This leaves the whole playground for press, publishing and journalism etc. another reason that encourages press or publishing to be augmented reality media is people's habits.

For example, some of us like of course to read their morning newspapers while having breakfast, so they use one hand for eating and the other for reading, the good news is they can use their both hands to eat while using an augmented reality book reader to read newspapers, of course virtual reality is not accepted here because the user is literally blind!

Nowadays some of us watch TV instead, so they can use their both hands to eat, the good news is this classic can be back using augmented reality book readers!

Another example, if you found some words on your breakfast that's OK even if you found some paragraphs it won't harm, but you will feel disgusting if one of those

Star Wars Jedi stepped on your breakfast, that's what's meant by people habits do force that augmented reality media is press or publishing, from the best practice point of view.

Although that major differences, there is some companies out there in the world trying to mix them together just as you do mix your own TV with your newspapers or just as you do mix apples and oranges, this is wrong, we are human beings we are not bots!

Augmented reality and virtual reality can be mixed only in theory because they both manufactured almost the same way from software engineering point of view, while they are both totally different as it's been explained from best practice point of view.

There are even some billionaires out there in the world trying to mix them too, because those companies or billionaires do not care about your safety or even a better world they only care about your money!

Each of virtual reality and augmented reality has a different future, the future of virtual reality is a new generation of TV sets of course while the future of augmented reality is a new generation of your book reader or may be a new generation of safety helmets or may be a new generation of cockpits, as it'll be explained later.

Mixing them together is really a social catastrophe, it will be explained as follows:

Now consider that your favorite virtual reality venue is going to be aired soon and you need to walk your chihuahua so badly. Do you dare to watch your favorite virtual reality venue (by wearing Oculus Go for example) while you are walking your chihuahua out? Could you walk your chihuahua and watch your Oculus Go, for example, while walking?

The answer is No of course for the most of you, Why? Because you won't look cool. Really, you are looking for troubles as you are literally blind while you are watching your favorite virtual reality venue! Of course, you can do so with a guide dog!

As we can see virtual reality best practice is to be used indoors as you do treat your own TV set, it's not suitable for outdoors! On the contrary, augmented reality is more suitable for outdoors, really when we use

augmented reality outdoors, we benefit its high precision while using augmented reality indoors is unnecessary most of the cases: what's the benefit of chasing
those Star Wars Jedi inside your house unless you need
to smash it because you are planning for redecoration?
Augmented reality can do better than a computer program or even a video game as it'll be explained later.

The Golden Safety Rules

Let us consider that you want to drive your car, what is the golden safety rules that you must follow?

Firstly, you must be sober, you can't drive your car while you are drunk.

Secondly, you must be 18 years or older, as stated by law.

Thirdly, you must have a driving license, that's to say you are a professional.

Those 3 golden safety rules for driving your car are essential, so you are aware of your own timeline at the current moment and you can make the right decision at the right moment also, this strategy reduces accidents to minimum. You should acquire a driving license to prove you can make the right decision at the right moment that's to say you are a professional.

Now consider you want to use your virtual reality or augmented reality device, what you need to reduce accidents to minimum?

Can you, virtual reality user or augmented reality user play your favorite game after drinking a large bottle of tequila? The answer is No of course for the most of you and this drives the following golden safety rules:

Firstly, you must be sober, you can't use your augmented reality device while you are drunk, or you might end up have fallen over your stairs, or even worse, you have fallen over your rooftop for some stupid game, neither have you jumped for love! This rule applies to virtual reality too, playing virtual reality while you are drunk means accidents, because while you are drunk, those guardian boundaries or safety boundaries that you have set won't help certainly.

Secondly, You must be 18 years or older, you can't use your augmented reality device outdoors if you are under 18 because you are not fully aware of your own current timeline besides you can't make the right decision at the right moment, if a person under 18 is using his augmented reality device outdoors, he might get hit and run by a car because he lacks the knowledge to make the right decision at the right moment. In other words, if you use your augmented reality device outdoors that means you are walking on the street without paying attention to your surrounding events. An over 18 persons might get hit and run by a car because they are walking on the street without paying attention to their surrounding events, what about those under 18 kids? For a virtual reality user, he must be 13 years or older, as stated by most virtual reality device manufactures because it's mostly used indoors!

Thirdly, you should be professional, you can't use your augmented reality device outdoors for the same reasons, you must be capable of making the right decision at the right moment! For a virtual reality user, this is not necessary because it's mostly used indoors!

To summarize those golden safety rules in a Hollywood style for simplicity: Virtual reality is a PG-13 movie while augmented reality is an R rated movie. Yes, this is the bitter truth: augmented reality is an R rated movie!

Those rules considered that you are following the best practice point of view, which is augmented reality for outdoors while virtual reality for indoors, but this is not the case if you are using your augmented reality device indoors. Using your augmented reality device indoors is bad practice but it's not forbidden, if you are using your augmented reality device indoors then you do neglect its high precision, as it'll be explained later, in most cases virtual reality is quite enough for indoors use.

The computer version of augmented reality is a modest version. When augmented reality is used to play a video game, that's a very modest version of augmented reality! In the next chapter the real power of augmented reality will be explained. So, you can understand the meaning of "modest version". What the "Virtual Reality and Augmented Reality Timeline Theory" is trying to do is to unleash the beast of augmented reality!

A Taste of Augmented Reality
Real Power

Before we discuss the social catastrophe arising due to mixing virtual reality and augmented reality together, let's point that one of augmented reality best practices is to be used as a gauge, it's explained here to emphasis the golden safety rules before we go on!

Let's take the case of a biker: a biker can't keep an eye on the speedometer or gasometer because it's difficult to look strait to watch the road and to look down to see the speedometer or gasometer. But the solution is augmented reality! How?

Simply the current reading of speedometer and gasometer can be both written on the glass or the lenses of the biker safety helmet using augmented reality technology, that's would save a lot of lives! That's the gauge I meant as a best practice for augmented reality, that's how the computer version of augmented reality is a modest version!

Of course, here we don't need every biker to get his eyes to be augmented reality implanted eyes like "The Terminator" because the safety helmet will do the trick! That's unleashing the true power of augmented reality. That's why we considered the case of that "you want to drive your car" previously, because the real guys for augmented reality are the drivers! That's why using augmented reality for a computer program or video game is a waste of precision and bad practice.

Also augmented reality is already there in your car! If your car has a rear camera so it does have augmented reality! Because those dotted lines that appears on the rear camera view are augmented reality, but car manufactures don't give augmented reality much attention! But if those companies which like to mix augmented reality and virtual reality together told them that you can technically program your car's rear camera to play Pokémon Go, this will draw their attention because this Pokémon car will sell crazy!

Technically, yes you can run the same Pokémon Go software on your car's rear camera for sure! So, you can play Pokémon Go on your car, your smartphone is not the only option!

The rest of augmented reality best practices will be explained later after firing the alarm to separate both virtual reality and augmented reality apart in the next chapter!

The Social Catastrophe

First, both virtual reality and augmented reality are a computer-generated view, this makes them both siblings from the software engineering point of view or in other words manufacturing point of view, that's to say if you have a virtual reality program, you can tweak it into augmented reality program easily, this introduced the idea of mixing them together! Although it's all wrong.

To explain the outcome of mixing virtual reality and augmented reality together as simply as possible we will adopt the Hollywood style version:

let's consider the case of "fifty shades of Grey" movie, this movie is starring Dakota Johnson and Eric Johnson who have no relation in-between, as they are both have the same last name "Johnson", so they must be siblings, and this concludes that "fifty shades of Grey" is a family movie! Yes, that's the conclusion if the same principals are applied to both cases!

Of course, you will exclaim because it's socially unaccepted to judge an R rated movie to be a family movie, because best practice point of view enforces that "fifty shades of Grey" is an R rated movie, but from production point of view it doesn't really matter if the movie even stars a husband and a wife, in other words a family movie. what really matters is the quality of the movie!

Socially, mixing both virtual reality and augmented reality is exactly as letting your kids who is under 18 watch "fifty shades of Grey". Because augmented reality is an R rated movie as mentioned previously, it's not the same as virtual reality. This mixture means they are both a PG-13 movie, but the truth is they are not!

Would you accept that your kids who are under 18 watch "fifty shades of Grey"?

The answer is no for the most of you, because "fifty shades of Grey" is an R rated movie. Really, we can't let the audience of virtual reality who are under 18 years old to be the audience of augmented reality whom must be 18 years old or older.

Really augmented reality is not a baby toy, it's not a game to play for fun this is a waste of precision, drivers are the real guys to use augmented reality as mentioned previously. Introducing augmented reality as a baby toy to everyone is mean really!

Virtual reality and augmented reality might use the same software as it is the case of an XBOX ONE device, the same software runs on your PC and on your game console too. But it's not definitely the same user.

Virtual Reality and Augmented Reality Best Practices

We'll explain in this chapter some virtual reality and augmented reality best practices:

Some best practices for virtual reality are movies, sports, video games or aerobics.

As mentioned before 6DoF virtual reality movies or 6DoF virtual reality music can be tailored to exercise aerobics correctly and can be monitored by a computer for coaching.

Some best practices for augmented reality are a book reader, GPS, gauges or medical endoscopy.

As previously discussed, an augmented reality book reader is socially accepted and welcomed more than a virtual reality book reader because if you found some words on your food that's OK, even if you found some paragraphs on your food, it won't harm, but you will feel disgusting if someone stepped on your food, as explained earlier.

As mentioned before a biker can't keep an eye on the speedometer or gasometer because it's difficult to look strait to watch the road and to look down to see the speedometer or gasometer.

But if the current reading of speedometer and gasometer both are written on the glass or the lenses of the biker safety helmet using augmented reality technology, that's would save a lot of lives! That's the gauge I meant as a best practice for augmented reality.

Also, the biker can get the name of the street he's driving through written on his safety helmet glass using augmented reality! That's would be very nice! That's the GPS I meant as best practice of augmented reality! That new generation of safety helmets is called unleashing the beast because that Star Wars Jedi game is a very tame version of augmented reality! Of course, this safety helmet may take years of development, but the "Virtual Reality and Augmented Reality Timeline Theory" is here to fire the alarm!

Also, the pilot's helmet can make use of augmented reality, a pilot can't keep an eye on cockpit's gauges because it's difficult to look strait to watch the sky and to look down to see the gauges. But the solution is augmented reality! How?

Simply the current reading of important gauges can be written on the glass or the lenses of the pilot's helmet using augmented reality technology, that's would mean a stronger cockpit! How?

Consider that the view of the surrounding sky is shown on the glass or the lenses of the pilot's helmet using cameras, we can use 50 cameras for example, those cameras get every angle of the surrounding sky, right then the cockpit has no use for windows, it can be windowless, but the obstacle until now is the pilot needs to see some important gauges in the cockpit! That's why there are no windowless cockpits nowadays. But the solution is augmented reality! How?

This obstacle can be overridden if the current reading of the important gauges is written on the glass or the lenses of the pilot's helmet using augmented reality technology while he gets the current view of the surrounding sky using cameras as described before! And that's how he can even lock on target, here, the pilot will be flying the airplane without looking at the control keys or knobs on the control panel exactly as a computer typist, she types on the keyboard without looking at it, this describes a windowless cockpit. Of course, this windowless cockpit may take years of development but the "Virtual Reality and Augmented Reality Timeline Theory" is here to fire the alarm!

This windowless cockpit is a breakthrough in aerospace industry because it's stronger than nowadays cockpits, it can be used in all kinds of air planes even private jets!

Let's say that if NASA has achieved this windowless cockpit then they can start building the Star Trek's USS Enterprise!

To make a long story short, the "Virtual Reality and Augmented Reality Timeline Theory" asks: why windows are used in cockpits to superimpose the view of the sky over the view of the instrument panel while this can be done electronically using augmented reality?

Now what about medical endoscopy:

Augmented reality can be used in medical endoscopy so that the doctor can get the name of the organ, which she's examining, written on the endoscope lenses. That would save lives as it would reduce human error chances.

Also, if the doctor can mark the beginning and the end of a tumor, for example, that she's examining using augmented reality, that would save lives as it would reduce human error chances.

Those examples are the true power of augmented reality, that's the beauty of augmented reality, that's unleashing the beast!

Standalone Augmented Reality Devices

As explained before, standalone augmented reality device is a bad practice, it's a waste of precision, but it's not forbidden. Any standalone augmented reality device project should be shut down because it lacks precision, it's the wrong type of business for augmented reality to play the rule of a PC.

Augmented reality should be part of another equipment to satisfy the third golden rule of safety which is the user should be a professional, for example: safety helmet or medical endoscopy etc.

Augmented reality should target the professional user not home user, augmented reality should target drivers, pilots, doctors or cops etc. Using augmented reality at home is exactly as using your own helicopter to visit your neighbors! That's too much, while using your own car to visit your neighbors is quite enough. In this case, what I meant by your car is virtual reality.

Besides, if you like to plan for decoration, business or presentation using augmented reality then don't, that's as too much as using your own helicopter to visit your neighbors! Because there is a cheaper option which is virtual reality. In most cases the virtual reality option is cheaper than the augmented reality option because augmented reality needs someone or some chip to make the right decision at the right moment, for your safety of course, and that means higher cost than virtual reality.

In general, augmented reality is more expensive than virtual reality! Virtual reality is the economic option for business presentation, decoration or house remake planning.

Oculus Quest

What's Oculus Quest? It's the new game console arriving in the US markets 2019. It's not a UFO, so nobody freaks out. It's the first true 3D game console with built-in screen. Others, like XBOX ONE or PlayStation, has no built-in screen.

Really, it's a huge leap forward in the game console industry and a strong competitor to PlayStation or other consoles, it should be called Oculus Console, But Oculus insists to choose names that insure nobody understands anything!

But should we call Oculus Quest a TV set? Absolutely not, a TV set can do more. For example, it displays the signal of your satellite decoder. I recommend buying Oculus Quest, so you can use it every morning, because some aerobics on every morning is a healthy habit!

Finally, I wish you all a happy virtual reality or augmented reality session.

PART TWO

Humanity Timeline Theory

Why a stone age man couldn't make himself an LCD, although LCD's raw material did exist at his time? The answer is a stone age man did not of course know how to make it, so he did not make himself an LCD. He did not even know how to turn sand into glass!

Why, unfortunately, do all nowadays airplanes have windows on their cockpits? The answer is airplane manufacturers do not know how to use augmented reality right. I bit they do not even know what it is!

So, the point is it's the "know how" that makes the difference between our modern age and the stone age! Yes, even a genius stone age man would be treated as a person with intellectual disability, if he came to our modern age!

Thus, the differences between human history timeline ages is all about the "know how" the more knowledge humanity has gathered the closer they are to our modern age, and vice versa! Now, humanity timeline theory is as follows:

Human history timeline ages are a scale of how much the humanity has accumulated of our modern age knowledge, the more knowledge humanity has gathered of our modern age knowledge the closer they are to our modern age, and vice versa!

The paragraph above is a social theory called "Humanity Timeline Theory" and that paragraph is about the broad human history timeline as a whole while the discussion about the single human timeline is called "Virtual Reality and Augmented Reality Timeline Theory"! For more information please read part one.

Now let's consider if someone managed to build a time travel machine in the year 2100AD and he traveled back one thousand years ago, would be his watch's date still 2100AD or not? The answer is yes, amazingly his watch would be still pointing to 2100AD although it would be 1100AD. How?

Because watches or clocks are just counters that count forward that's to say 1,2,3, ...etc. and it happens by coincidence that this count matches the right time, yes surprisingly there are no strings attached between your watch and human history timeline of course! That time traveler really would need to set his watch again to 1100AD because his watch is just a forward counter that counts seconds forward only! It's the same thing even if he used an atomic clock.

Alas, there is no known device to determine where you are on the human history timeline! Even an atomic clock is not suitable for time travel!

This leads to the only known way to determine where you are on the human history timeline is the human mind judgment on the sequence of events he had previously. That's to say: your position on the human history timeline is only judged by your mind! How?

Let's consider that back-time traveler, his watch is useless of course, so he will try to calculate how much people around him have accumulated of his age's knowledge, that's to say he will compare that age's humanity knowledge to his age's humanity knowledge which is our modern age. the more knowledge those people around him have gathered of our modern age's knowledge the closer they are to our modern age, and vice versa! As stated by "Humanity Timeline Theory".

Simply, "Humanity Timeline Theory" explains how our minds do judge our position through human history timeline.

In simple words, if that back-time traveler saw people around him riding cars to go to work, he would think that his time travel machine has failed but if he saw them riding horses to go to work, he would think his time travel machine has succeeded!

Now let's consider if someone managed to build a time travel machine in the year 2100AD and traveled forward one thousand years, would be his watch's date still 2100AD or not? The answer is yes, amazingly his watch would be still pointing to 2100AD although it would be 3100AD. How?

Because his watch is just a forward counter that counts seconds forward only! It's the same thing even if he used an atomic clock. It does not leap seconds or years, that time traveler really would need to set his

watch again to 3100AD because there are no strings attached between his watch and human history timeline
of course!

Now that forward time traveler would need to calculate how much people around him have accumulated
of his age's knowledge, that's to say he will compare that
age's humanity knowledge to his age's humanity knowledge which is our modern age. The more knowledge
those people around him have gathered of our modern
age's knowledge the closer they are to our modern age!

In simple words, if that forward time traveler saw
people around him riding cars to go to work, he would
think that his time travel machine has failed but if he
saw them riding UFOs to go to work, he would think his
time travel machine has succeeded!

But if that forward time traveler saw people around
him riding horses to go to work, he would think that his
time travel machine has failed. Although, it really would
be 3100AD and people around him are riding horses to
go to work because a nuclear war that took place some-
time before 3100AD, this nuclear war has taken every

known technology to the ground! As you can see using mind judgment to exactly determine your human history timeline position is tricky!

I hope this theory will be the first step for inventing a time travel machine because a better understanding of the problem always helps to find a solution to that problem. I have not seen serious steps taken to build a time travel machine although the modern technology is so close to building one! For further reading, I recommend the book "Known Facts of Time Travel" which discusses "Humanity Timeline Theory" in more details.

Finally, I wish you all a happy time travel trip.

Don't miss out!

Visit the website below and you can sign up to receive emails whenever Mohammed Azzam publishes a new book. There's no charge and no obligation.

https://books2read.com/r/B-A-QOZG-NLFV

BOOKS 2 READ

Connecting independent readers to independent writers.

Also by Mohammed Azzam

Inflation and Variable Interest
Virtual Reality and Augmented Reality Safety Rules
Known Facts of Time Travel

Watch for more at https://books2read.com/ap/
R3Lm35/Mohammed-Azzam.

About the Author

Hello, my name is Mohammed Azzam :
E–Mail : smartspecies@hotmail.com
Occupation : software-engineer.
Education : Faculty of Engineering - I have a B.A. in Automatic Control Engineering.
Certification :
Oracle PL/SQL Developer Certified Associate (OCA)
Oracle Forms Developer Certified Professional (OCP)
Oracle Database: SQL Certified Expert (OCE) Oracle Certified Professional, Java SE 6 Programmer (SCJP)
Oracle Certified Expert, Java EE 6 Web Component

Developer (SCWCD)
Read more at https://books2read.com/ap/
R3Lm35/Mohammed-Azzam.

9 781726 824248